t

SOMETHING WITHIN

SOMETHING
WITHIN

Reflections and Sketches by
NOLLAIG O'DONNELL

VERITAS

Published 2016 by
Veritas Publications
7–8 Lower Abbey Street
Dublin 1
Ireland
publications@veritas.ie
www.veritas.ie

ISBN 978 1 84730 748 4

10 9 8 7 6 5 4 3 2 1

Designed by Padraig McCormack, Veritas Publications
Printed in Ireland by Anglo Printers, Drogheda

Veritas books are printed on paper made from the wood pulp of managed forests. For every tree felled, at least one tree is planted, thereby renewing natural resources.

Pour le Sacré-Coeur

Contents

Be A Child

Let me be a child –

Heart's deep root of love to prize;

Winging only good.

Park Retreat

Public park retreat:
Figure poised o'er fountain rush –
Chiselled into hush.

At Last I Met My Friend Today

At last I met my friend today –
We hadn't met – He'd been away.
A meeting warm, with smiles at first –
Turned fast to talk – I thought I'd burst!

'My friend,' I said, 'You've let me down.
You didn't call – You weren't around.
In recent times, my spirits fell.
My friend,' I asked, 'could you not tell?'

The silence hung between us there;
I thought – my friend – he did not care.
The pain and hurt of friend forgot,
Had laid their weight – I grew distraught.

Just then, my friend, he reached inside
A little bag left by his side.
From it he drew a special token:
'A gift for you – feel free to open!'

'It seems,' he said, 'you can't rely,
I wasn't there, I can't deny.
Yet on my treks, where'er I've been –
I keep in mind those of my kin!'

Waiting

Waiting can be oh-so-boring for some; like a long, languid sigh; an empty space in time, where sounds mix and mingle in a meaningless cacophony.

For others, waiting is gadget-fidget-clock-watching time; an opportunity to raise the blood pressure and lose the head; to worry the hurry into a flurry of dread.

For me, waiting is skating on ice to the strains of 'Für Elise' – a time to glide and slide, to whirl and twirl; to watch and catch the glances, the rhythms and cadences in conversations shared; or, on occasion, waiting is simply to peel the silence and savour its juices, mindfully.

Song of the Prom

A walk on the prom brings calm to the mind.

Hear the steps on the way tread the cares of the day.

See the breeze toss the sand bring a tear to your eye.

Smell the sea in the air – deep breath in and exhale.

Hear the sound of your heart in the beat of the waves. Let the song of the birds bring a smile to your face.

Pass the swings in the green; catch the kids and their screams.

Take that break from the strife of your everyday life.

Summer Breakfast

I wake to the long day ahead …
I stretch and trust to be led …
Hear a siren screech fear
Shrill an ache in my ear –
Till the song of a bird
Brings me home to the Word!
Watch the sun-faded drapes
Hang a frown on my face –
Till the leaves on the trees
Dance a shade in the breeze.
Smell the bread in the air –
Deep breath in … and exhale …
Touch my lips with a slice,
Makes me smile in a trice!
Now my tastebuds arrived –
I thank God – I'm alive!

Flower Power

Windowsill aglow
Bellafonte purrs in awe –
Flower power in the sun!

Heaven-Scent

Lake-side Heaven-scent;

Weeping-willow dips its toe –

Ripples into heart.

November

In this month of November,
We take time to remember
Those whose lives touched our lives –
Those whose smiles touched our hearts.

For our loved ones gone before, Lord,
you open wide your door.
In your care, we place our people –
All the living and the dead.

Past Present to the Future

'Would you mind coming over to the house?' he asks. 'There's a meeting on here now, so I've got to move out.'

'No problem,' I say.

It's late September and it's getting late. I've just returned from Nice, tanned and relaxed. We chat about my holidays. As we reach the back door, I feel a sense of excitement building inside of me. And, just as he leans on the door handle, he says he hopes I'm not too tired to have this meeting now, given that I've been travelling all day. Just then I realise how much of myself I have already invested in this project; how it had resonated with me and gripped my heart the first time he had mentioned it. The apprehension is still there and a little fear lurks in the background, but is well diluted by his gift of complete confidence in me. And, as for being tired, no, I am definitely not tired.

As the glass door seems to glide into the kitchen, all the possibilities of a new life open before me ...

Dark Dialogue

'A gift,' he said.

'A blight!'

'A chance to better see,' he said.

'Dark night!'

'Obscurity surrounds,' he said.

'Take flight!'

'That silent deep distils,' he said.

'It might.'

'The dread and fear – it kills,' he said.

'That's right.'

'Brings the chambers of the heart ...' he said.

'In sight ...'

'And there, within, Dark shines ...'

'A Light!'

Night Time

The sun is done – the dark has won.

And rest, the light king must.

The birds have shown – their flight they've flown;

To nest, their place of rest.

The flower knows it's time to close;

Its head in slumber bows.

No craze of life – that daylight strife

Should in the dark be found.

Yet, desperately, we cling to hours

That met and had their day.

We burn the light that hides the night;

We work the day till night turns bright.

We fear the silent moonbeam's way –

Her nudge to hear what dark might say.

And yet, to night time, one and all
Must heed the call – must take the fall.
A brighter day will follow when,
With light, we've made the dark our friend.

Time and Tide

Sun, sea-sound, boats click.
Book and bike on Spiddal pier –
Time and tide are mine.

Advent

Where is the hope
In long, dark days?
No light, nor heat
To lift the soul –
Ere joyful hearts 'n grateful nations
Rejoice in Christmas Day once more!

The Senses Allowed

We don't need words to hear the birds;
Nor touch to feel the pain;
No lens to spot the stars by night,
Or watch the falling rain.

We don't need texts to send our thoughts;
No e-mails to the cloud.
No need to run – we walk instead
To taste the world aloud!

Black and White

Fingertips in flight –
Swift, sonorous, dark and bright
Play on black and white.

Hope in Slumber

Growing in motion;
Cupped in slumber – changing oft.
Hope and hold aloft.

Being!

Swirling on scan caught;

Carved on palm and ne'er forgot.

Being – there's a thought!

In Memory of Bells

A crib retreat in candle light;
A stable – roof and walls.
A star o'er head smiles at the sight,
On golden branches falls.

An angel stands aloft the crib,
The Christmas scene beholds.
A book in hands respectful bears
A Testament to hope.

The Saviour's cradle gently rocks
A soothing to and fro;
While kneeling, Mary's poised to sing
Her baby sweet and low.

The shepherds, sheep – the black and white! –
The ox and donkey fill
A breath, with love, to warm the child –
A joy in us instils.

And now my inner eye delights
Through time in silence shared;
The crib, the star – my heart ignites!
While bells ring call to prayer.

By the Fire

My dearest childhood memories of warmth and wonder have as their backdrop our dining room fireplace ... I'm eight years old, sitting at the dining room table, colouring. I'm facing a glorious turf fire. Mam is sitting by the fire, reading the newspaper. Dada is singing 'Oklahoma' in the kitchen while washing the dishes. It's a moment of domestic bliss, a scene poised to be punctured!

The dining room door opens. 'Time for the Rosary,' says Dada entering the room. 'Put away the colouring,' Mam smirks as she catches his wink. 'Aw! No Dada,' I protest. 'I'll only be two more minutes. I just have to colour in the glass of milk.' 'Colour in the glass of milk!' says Dada. 'You're working on a white background there – I'd say your glass of milk is already coloured in! And even if your picture isn't finished, remember the story of the little girl who was doing her homework and when she was called to say the Rosary, she dropped her pen immediately and joined in the Rosary only to find that when she returned to her homework, it had been finished for her by an angel, and written in gold.'

I loved hearing that story and I knew that, like every story Dada told, it was true, regardless of whether or not it had actually ever happened. Mam put another sod of turf in the fire. I pushed my chair in front of the fire and knelt down, leaning my elbows on the seat of the chair and looking into the warm flames. 'The Lord shall open my lips,' said Dada. 'And my tongue shall announce Thy praise,' Mam and I continued … as I imagined the angel struggling to colour in my glass of milk with her gold pen!

Heart and Soul

Break-through in the haze;

A clarity unbidden –

Heart and soul are one.

Catedral
de
Santiago.

Daybreak in Santiago

Change – a day away:

Chance to find the life in years.

Daybreak for the soul.

Gift of Present Time

Gift of present time:

Rolling waves unfold a sea –

Rhythmical, calm.

My Soul Grows Deep
like the Rivers

I almost say ... then I don't ... I stop short. You make me listen. You always do. And in listening, I am learning, and what I am learning is acceptance. Just as I am about to wade in with words of 'wisdom' born of living life slightly out of focus; you click and – hey presto! – you take the shot. I'm left reeling in the years. I'm forced to reassess harsh wisdom and old taboos. The challenge is to change; and in the change, my soul grows deep like the rivers.

Divinely Idyllic

A cycle path through the heart of the Normandy countryside – destination Giverny …

'Monet's garden – funny you should mention it,' he'd said. 'Someone was talking about it just the other day and I thought, "That's somewhere I'd love to visit," – he stalled – 'before I leave.'

I knew at that moment that this would indeed be the highlight of my visit to France – our trip to the heart of one artist's vision of Heaven on earth.

It is now mid-afternoon. We're sitting in the outdoor, picket-fence encircled tea shop at the perimeter of the paradise that is Monet's garden. Having first enjoyed the guided tour – savoured the scent of a myriad of flowers; sat at the water's edge; crossed the Japanese bridge; admired the water lilies – we finally sauntered through the master's great pink house to relish, once again, his glorious garden,

but, this time, through the artist's eye and palette. We are now ready for a cuppa!

We sit facing each other across an impossibly tiny, round table, choc-a-bloc with floral daintiness – just the spot for a heart to open up and declare itself – and so it did:

'Art is about beauty,' he said, 'beauty that touches the heart. Otherwise, what's the point?'

Soundless Noise

Being well appraised of, and knowing everything;
And I – no wiseacre at all,
Feel diminished in their presence;
In their chatter – golden silence cannot fall.

Their words throng every moment of our meeting;
Their talk, advice and certainties.
I, shutting down, turn inward;
Immobilised by memories.

Thus sparks many reminiscences
Of a time when this began;
My self-expression was in painting,
And playing piano for the clan.

Thus, this art-filled world of colour,
Oft enhanced by writing skill,
Would eschew the tiresome chatter
Of their strident rumour mill.

But now, amid the musings,
A notion rich in insight springs –
Are tacit judgements just as noisy
As their vocal jabberings?

To Live the Book

I choose to read to save my soul;
In full control I'll be –
Take my book to a quiet nook
And therein find the key.

And so I delve into the depths;
Scale the heights, cross the seas.
Dreams and schemes of other people –
No cause of fear for me.

Adventures and advice, I read;
Science and poetry.
The sacred Scriptures – yes – the Word!
I study avidly.

And then, one day, the book takes life;
Fate sends a trial to me.
With reading done, and wisdom won –
No challenge should this be.

But oh, the shock! – the cross to lift;
The pain, the cup to drink.
The printed word – no substitute –
No passion flares in ink!

Spirit Level

Dense morning mist chill

Tests the spirit – checks the will:

Hope's weight in water.

Light Flight

Kite in flight to light holds tight,
In sun's rays, weaves and dips.
Height o'er might soars to the light,
In freedom lets it rip!

Kite at night; no light to site –
Recoils, retreats and sways.
Light to blighted kite ignite! –
Encircle all our days.

The Piano Lesson

Adam has just played a dodgy rendition of the last few bars of his exam piece for the third time and, in the process, has exhausted his attention span. In response to this, he swings around on the piano stool, jumps off and dives under the desk behind us.

'I don't think you've met Dutch,' he says, emerging, clutching the most purringly handsome grey cat imaginable.

'Wow! He's gorgeous,' I say, falling, yet again, for another of Adam's devious distractions. 'But why "Dutch"?' I ask.

'Because my little brother can't pronounce "Judge",' he says.

I don't enquire any further into that particular mystery.

Next thing I know, the door to the 'music room' is flung open by Freddy, the two-year-old little brother – one of four siblings, any one of whom Adam is likely to call his 'little brother.'

'Mom is home!' comes the rallying cry from the hall. Freddy's summons to all the little troops to halt, call a truce – however temporary! – and descend on 'Mom' with a warm and wild céad míle fáilte.

Only Adam does not stir. He looks on, holding Dutch. He is, after all, the 'big brother.' I can sense his internal struggle.

'How about we get back to work for our last ten minutes,' I suggest to break the impasse.

It works. Adam settles Dutch back under the desk and we resume the piano lesson, the backdrop to this boy's first step into manhood.

Wendy

I'm standing in the hall with Wendy and Joe. The four boys have just had their piano lessons and I'm about to leave.

'I hope they're not giving you any trouble,' Joe says. 'I know they can be "lively".'

'No,' I say, 'not at all. They are good as gold!'

Both he and Wendy throw me a knowing glance and we all enjoy the lie!

Wendy opens the front door for me and strolls outside with me to my car.

'I heard you met Dutch,' she says.

'Oh! Yes,' I enthuse. 'He's a gorgeous cat!'

'Yeah!' says Wendy, 'the boys love Dutch – so does Joe. We're all mad about Dutch – but, you know, in our house,' she stalled for a moment, 'even the cat is male.' And, pointing back inside, she adds, 'I'm on my own in there.'

'In gender only, Wendy,' I say, 'only in gender.'

I am Red Riding Hood

I'm layers and layers of cares and flares –
An onion, if you will.
My outer dress, I must confess,
Was never meant to thrill.

The hood, the cape, the bow at nape –
A wounded wolf conceal.
But oh! the chance to peel and lance
The blistered heart to heal.

Coffee and Spirits

I met two friends for coffee-break –
The dearest friends I know;
The clock – its busy hands forgot –
We jump! 'It's time to go!'

Our haven, warm, we leave behind,
And steel ourselves for bitter climes;
And now to face those busy streets –
To open door on wind that sweeps.

To walk, as one, a sharing step
Draws closer parting from my self.
I sense their spirits strike me deep:
The one did bounce – the other seep.
As words do flow – our heads incline –
Like time in prayer – our souls align.

The Truth of the Imagination

What view is this? What do I see?
The water flows beside the trees.
The mountains rise from blue lake's edge.

My gaze ascends this mixed-green wedge.

And standing high on mountain top,
My mind stands tall – my thoughts to stop.

I face the breeze; my eyelids drop.

I taste the water in the air.
I hear the birds – their call to pair.
I stoop to touch the rugged grass.
I feel the Earth in my small grasp.

And, opening wide my eyes once more –
I find I haven't left the shore.

To ford the lake, and scale the heights;
Imagination will, in truth,
Take flight!

Play is Life!

Share a joke, a cry;

Chatter, natter, howling laugh –

Children's play is life!

Lent

A faith retreat in Easter light;
Forty days to set things right.
Repent, believe and pay attention –
A desert route to conversion.

A hope retreat in Easter light;
In trust, our God, we keep in sight.
Our faults and failings, you forgive,
Which wakes our joy and lets us live.

A love retreat in Easter light;
With Christ, we walk through His dark night;
The road to Easter celebration –
Our door to Christian liberation.

All for One

Silent cycle track –
Just the click of friendships pass.
All for one to last.

Ease

I can feel the wind in my face. I'm running by the sea. I hear the birds sing. I'm smiling. The water's edge; the sun on the sea; the clouds drifting by; no stopping, no waiting, no longing – just being! Easy, airy being in this present moment – no attending to the last or to the next. 'Now' is all there is.

I'm writing with ease, with great ease. Ideas come with ease. The pen flows over paper with ease. The words smile as I dot in the 'eyes' and swing upwards the ink-flow into smile. I start the process of writing … and next thing I know, it is underway – the way becomes clear – the characters know themselves. They have to become clear in me. After that, they're my friends and I'm at ease with them. We confide in each other. I know them deeply and care for all of them as though each one is a part of me – which they are. Nothing scary. Nothing to hold me back – easeful.

Rainbow Song

Can a rainbow sing?

Colour captures everything.

Listen deep within.

I Am Standing in a Doorway

To my right, the familiar, heavy, cream-panelled door with the shaky gold, over-polished doorknob. On the floor in front of me and to my left, long rectangles of light – the dining room carpet in faded panels.

'I think it's time to get a new carpet, Mam,' I suggest. 'This one's seen the light a little too long!'

'That carpet will last for as long as I'll need it,' Mam replies, adding, 'I'll e-mail you my opinion on the next one from "beyond",' pointing a long index finger slowly upwards, then downwards, followed fleetingly by a raised eyebrow, a stifled smirk and an impish glint in her eye.

For someone so reserved, so reticent, so slow to move outside her own space – going 'beyond' never bothered her in the least. 'It'll be a great experience,' she would say. We often laughed about it.

Did I ever, ever dream that standing there on that day, in that doorway, in that light on 19 April 2010, that this would be our very last time here together?

Riddle of the Garden

Riddle me a garden mystery,
With a lake-side, ring-side view.
Reflect, in the water before me,
The spell of the garden anew.

Mountains surrounding its vista
Rise to a heavenly blue.
Their majesty lends to the secret
A charm that is ancient and new.

Inside its tree-lined defences
Lies a myriad of colours to woo.
Their scent, all day long, fills the senses;
Their breath, like the soft morning dew.

I go, like a sleuth, to the garden;
A vast celebration to view.
Diversity flowered into blossom;
Assorted their colours in hue.

This garden has spoken its secret;
Its memory none can undo.
Its mystery shared with the many;
United, divergent and true.

Swelling Sails

Sun-drenched bay at noon.
Swelling sails swooning windward;
Hooker high on tide.

Draw a Breath

Hear and heed bird song.

Restful calm – the evening's long.

Draw a breath; stay young.

Elemental Life

Fog's grey density –

Weight of water: heavy, still.

Elemental life.

Light-Time Experience

The light from the crescent moon casts a warm glow over the whitewashed cottage. I approach with a determined step. My internal compass, preset, has guided me here.

I hold the door handle steady in my hand as I push open into another life. The apprehension within is mounting. My heart rate increases with every moment. And then, there before me, bathed in soft moonlight is my piano – straight and upright, standing against the wall – facing me as I enter. And just overhead is a tiny, rectangular window, through which the moon pushes her light.

I sit at the piano. My favourite piece, 'The Tree of Life', is open before me. I start to play. I am filled with an overwhelming sense of peace and calm. My body sways to the rhythm. I am home!

A New Heart of Love

Old heart of stone, we leave behind –
New heart of flesh, instead, we find.
The heart that You, for us, reserve
Is one of love – We go and serve!

Cloud-Burst

Cloud-burst of seven

Daze, a weaker mind says 'No':

Come reign of heaven.

The Heart Apart

In parting, the heart will not play by the rules.
In parting, the heart makes its own set of tools.
The taking, the breaking, the fear and the pain:
In waking, in waiting, in prayer – not in vain.

A Time to Share

Who cares if sharing's day is gone;
Who knows if caring's time is done;
What place then, 'being there' for one –
When all, and time itself, have run?

I see, in deed, a need to share;
To open wide our heart of care;
To set in stone our word – declare
What's deep inside our soul – lay bare.

Spin

Pack book, rug and tuck –
Cycle-ride to the ocean;
Spin – prayer in motion!

Easter People!

A supper in the upper room.
The mystery of an empty tomb.
A tale of grief, death, fear and pain.
Is Jesus gone? – Our hope in vain?
We foolish people – slow to trust;
Are homeward bound – despondent, crushed;
Meet the stranger, whose words inspire –
Soul companion – our hearts on fire!
Stranger invited as our guest –
Stranger as host – our home is blest.
Bread is broken – Himself He gives:
Our eyes are open – our Saviour lives!

Camino Trail

Fresh Camino trail;

With burning heart my soul sings –

Recognisable.

Soar

Let the eagle soar,
In the Lord's limitless sky,
Flying with His wings.

Exam Time

Nerves at fever pitch ...

A prayer ... Gallows-headed frown.

Count-down's over – Write!

Pause

Lights bright, music soft –
Coffee maker clack and whack:
Mindful pause in sight!

Shadowman

Shadowman follows me
Wherever I go.
He stops when I stop.
He goes when I go.
When I stand in the desert
Of far-distant lands –
My shadowman watches.
He stands where I stand.

In the day-light, I set out –
In the morning-mist chill;
No sunshine – no shadows –
A long day uphill.
But, later, before me,
In the clearing below –
A pilgrim treads softly;
Shadowman in tow.

The afternoon leads me
To converse with my friend
Of burdens we carry,
Of ways we would mend.
Till a leaf floating gently
From a branch, in a puff,
Lays to rest on its shadow –
A sign from above.

In the evening, my shadowman
Lengthens his spectre.
He stretches before me;
My step – his director.
Just then, leaf and pilgrim –
Their shadows and mine –
Prove our shadowman's with us –
His presence divine!

Pentecost

Let's celebrate, this Pentecost,
That God still works among us.
His Holy Spirit gives us gifts
That we may carry out His work.

So, it's with joy we heed our calling
As God's people in His kingdom;
Our time as His disciples –
Renewed of purpose and of hope!

Gratitude

Jesus, for your love, we thank you –
For your presence in our lives;
Through your forgiveness and compassion –
We become one of your kind.

Thank you, Lord, for every blessing –
For all graces – old and new;
A grateful heart – just and respectful –
Yet another gift from you.

Gratitude gives new awareness –
A new freedom deep within:
Free to love in God's creation –
Free to rest in peace with Him.

Acknowledgements

To my late parents, Maudie and Seán Guinane, who were the inspiration for so much of this book, I owe an enormous debt of gratitude. My thanks to Mam for passing on her creative streak, as well as for her wit and wisdom; and to Dada, for lighting candles with me all those years ago, and for sharing his sense of the divine. My thanks to both of them for their unconditional love.

To Richard – thank you for your encouragement, and for committing my poems to memory and reciting them to me – I must get around to learning them myself some time!

I would also like to thank Harry and Meena for your support and for believing in this project. And a very special thanks to Seán for your ever-present smile and for the laughter that is a mark of our faith.

A very special word of thanks to all my wonderful friends who have helped me, in so many ways, to bring this book to completion.